I0099145

The Power of Rejection

Ayannah Williams

Copyright © 2016 Ayannah Williams

All rights reserved. No portion of the book may be reproduced or utilized in any form or by any means, electronic or mechanical, including photocopying, recording, or by any other information storage and retrieval system, without permission in writing from the author.

FOREWORD

By: Doug Williams

Gospel Recording Artist and CEO of Blackberry Records, Inc.

In a society like the one we live in today, where so many people are lost, confused, distraught and sad, it brings me great joy to know that there are some people who have been enlightened, empowered and have found an inner peace that surpasses all understanding. One such person is the author of this book, my daughter, Ayannah Williams. From the time she was a small child, I always knew that there was something special and unique about her. With such a humble spirit, a kind heart and a real love for people, there was a certain Godliness about her at a very early age. I did not know at that time how God would use her, but I felt in my heart that He would one day use her for His glory. Like many of us, Ayannah has gone through some difficult and trying times in her life. She has endured pain, disappointments, heartbreak and letdowns, but through prayer and her unyielding faith in God, she withstood every test and trial and is now a true witness for God. She has been anointed by God, appointed and called to preach the Gospel to a sin sick world. Ayannah has overcome the attacks of the enemy by the blood of the Lamb and by the word of her testimony. Her messages come from a very real place, and I am a firm believer that what comes from the heart, reaches the heart. I am so grateful for this awesome Woman of God and I am tremendously proud to call her my daughter. May you be blessed by the words in this book.

TABLE OF CONTENTS

"SALVATION- A FREE GIFT"

Scripture: "That if thou shalt confess with thy
mouth the Lord Jesus, and shalt believe in thine
heart that God hath raised him from the dead,
thou shalt be saved. For with the heart man
believeth unto righteousness; and with the mouth
confession is made unto salvation."
Romans 10:9-10

"Repent, and be baptized every one of you in the
name of Jesus Christ for the remission of sins,
and ye shall receive the gift of the Holy Ghost."
Acts 2:38

Are you saved? If you died at this moment, are you confident that you would spend eternity with Christ? If you are not sure, then TODAY is your day! The most important decision you will ever make in your life is to give your life to Jesus Christ. The whole purpose of our earthly existence is to be in fellowship with God. He desires a close relationship with YOU. Jesus died so that you could live a life free from the bondage of sin and death. When you accept Jesus into your heart, you receive a new beginning, a fresh start and a brand new way of living. All you have to do is believe! Are you ready to receive Christ now? Say this prayer out loud as your confession that you believe.

PRAYER OF SALVATION

Dear Jesus, I believe You are the Son of God. I believe You died for me on the cross and shed Your innocent blood for my sins. I believe that God raised You from the dead on the third day and You are now seated at the right hand of the Father. I recognize that I am a sinner and I repent of my sins. Please forgive my sins and wash me with Your blood. Come into my heart. Save my soul as I give my life to You. I make You my Lord and Savior. Fill me with Your Holy Spirit. I will now live the rest of my life for You. I am born again. In the name of Jesus, Amen.

You did it! You are saved! The Bible declares that when one sinner repents, the angels of God rejoice (Luke 15:10)! Second Corinthians 5:17 states, "Therefore if any man be in Christ, he is a new creature: old things are passed away; behold, all things are become new." You are brand new! Welcome to the Kingdom of GOD!

"THE POWER OF REJECTION"

INTRODUCTION

A few years ago while sitting in a minister's meeting with my pastor, he asked a question to all of the ministers in attendance. His question was thought provoking and deep. "What group of people are you called to minister to?" he asked. Quietly in my mind I said, "I'm called to the Rejected." Why would I think that? What made me feel that as a minister I would effectively be able to minister to people who have been rejected? The answer is simple; I have been rejected. Honestly, after writing this book, what I thought were some of the worst cases of rejection that I have ever encountered turned out to be some of the best experiences that could have ever happened for me. Keep in mind that I said "for me" and not "to me". JESUS is the best thing that ever happened "to me", but rejection happened "for me". What do I mean by this statement? In this book, which was birthed from a painful place of rejection, you will be able to see the powerful side of rejection and why God allows it to happen. Are you ready? Let's go!

Rejection is defined as the act of not accepting, refusing to have, casting out or ejecting. Synonymously, rejection can also mean to cast aside, dismiss, shun, throw away, forsake, deny, separate, brush-off, be cold towards and even to walk out on, just to name a few. It is closely related to the word "ostracize" which means to exclude, avoid and abandon. I have read many articles that gave the negative, downside of rejection. The truth is, rejection can be extremely painful and possibly detrimental, but I noticed something that was always consistent in every situation where I was rejected, and this was that each situation pushed me to a higher place in God. Rejection ultimately kept me out of places that God prohibited me to be in. There was never a time in my life that God did not use the pain and process of rejection to bless me. When I think of all the times I was rejected by friends and loved ones, and even by those who hardly knew me, I now consider it an honor to have been rejected. Yes, an honor! Psalm 119:71 (KJV) says, *"It is good for me that I have been afflicted; that I might learn thy statutes."* Rejection allowed me to see the strength inside of me and it pushed me to trust in and lean on God totally. Though I felt rejected and isolated, I was never alone; God was always with me.

As I look back over my life, I realize that God was with me even from my mother's womb. The shocking part is, God even gave me my name "Ayannah", and He gave you your name as well. How do I know this? One day while sitting on my living room floor reading my Bible, God led me to Luke Chapter 1. In this chapter, the angel of the Lord by the name of Gabriel appeared to Zacharias as he was at the altar in the Temple of the Lord. Gabriel told Zacharias that his wife Elisabeth shall bear a son and shall call his name "John". In that same chapter, the angel of the Lord, Gabriel, was sent to the virgin Mary and spoke these words to her: *"Thou shalt conceive in thy womb, and bring forth a son, and shalt call his name JESUS"* (verse 31). That is when the revelation hit me! God named me! Also, the same thing happened for you, that even as a seed in your mother's womb, God had a name for you as well as a plan for your life. Psalm 139:16 (NLT) David declares, *"You saw me before I was born. Every day of my life was recorded in your book. Every moment was laid out before a single day had passed."* This means that from beginning to the end, God laid out a specific plan for your life. The point I am trying to make is that if God knows your name, then God knows your pain and He knows exactly where you are.

All of my life I have never been able to fit in. Even today in my young adult life, I have never had many friends. Oftentimes, I would look at myself and say, "It must be me." I have tried to fit in; I have tried to make people like me; I have bought gifts; I have gone out of my way; I did things from the kindness of my heart; and yet, people rejected me. I have often felt that I gave out way more than what I got in return, not to mention that I have always had a hard time letting people go. Can you relate? When I love people, I love them wholeheartedly and when they decide to leave, it hurts. I try always to be genuine, loyal and faithful and I will never change this about myself. Yet, I have been rejected. With all honesty, I have loved people who just did not love me back. I would often ask God, "Why is it so hard for me to let people go?" So then I would try to shelter myself and put walls up and guard my heart. I would say, "I'm not letting anybody else get that close to me to hurt me." But the truth is, God does not want us to live in a sheltered box. As Saints in the body of Christ, we need each other. However, I have learned that no matter how people treat me, I am commanded by God to love and to forgive. There has to be a Judas somewhere in your life, and he has to get close enough to kiss you. Do you understand what I am saying spiritually? God will allow some things to happen in your life to test you to your inner core. It is necessary; it is just Kingdom business. I have experienced rejection in my family; rejection in ministry; rejection on jobs; and the list goes on. However, God has always used every situation to better me, to grow me up, to mature me and to prepare me for what is ahead. Rejection is a part of the preparation process for where you are headed. Let's go deeper!

CHAPTER 1

"THE REALITY OF REJECTION"

Rejection comes in many forms and circumstances. Some of you may have experienced the rejection of an absent mother or father, the rejection of friends and loved ones, rejection on a job, rejection from certain groups or rejection from the world. You have to recognize that when incidents such as rejection take place, the experience allows you to share in the same sufferings as Christ did. The Bible describes Jesus as being the stone that the builders rejected, and that same stone has now become the chief cornerstone (Psalm 118:22). Rejection is a major part of our Christian walk with Christ. The Bible declares in John 1:11 (KJV) *"He (Jesus) came unto his own, and his own received him not."* You may even recall that Judas betrayed Jesus and Peter denied Jesus three times. These men were extremely close to Jesus and yet they rejected Him. So count it all joy that you have experienced rejection because now you can identify with Christ, our Savior. Not only can you identify with Christ, but the Bible tells us that *"we have not an high priest which cannot be touched with the feeling of our infirmities"* (Hebrews 4:15 KJV), which means, Christ can identify with you also.

The truth about rejection is that if we do not see rejection from a Godly standpoint, then we give room to the enemy to bring spirits such as hurt, fear, sadness, hopelessness, anxiety, depression, loneliness, lust, low self-esteem and even suicide. Please trust me when I say I have experienced all of those. Now I am not saying that you will not feel the sting of rejection, but after reading this book, I decree and declare in the name of Jesus that we take the power away from the enemy and begin giving God glory for every situation in which we have experienced or will experience rejection. Regardless of the circumstance, I want you to know that it is working together for your good.

The way to overcome rejection is to realize that there is power in rejection and that God has ALLOWED it for a specific purpose in your life. Do not cry when people reject you. Celebrate the fact that God is leading and guiding you and that He knows what is best for you. Rejection is a sign that God does not want you in a particular place.

That place does not fit the perfect plan that He has for your life. Galatians 5: 7-8 (NLT) states, *"You were running the race so well. Who has held you back from following the truth? It certainly isn't God, for He is the one who called you to freedom."* Rejection is sent to redirect you to the people, places and things that God has for you. It is an indication that you have outgrown that level and realm that you are in. Think of a baby in a mother's womb. After nine months, her womb no longer has the capacity to carry that baby. The womb has served its purpose. Rejection is a sure sign that those people, places or things have served their purpose and no longer have the natural or spiritual capacity and ability to properly handle you and where you are going. That place is too small for you. The mindset of those people will hinder you. That atmosphere will stunt your growth. When you begin to stay in a place too long or get too comfortable around the wrong people or in the wrong places, God sends rejection as a signal that it is time to move on. So rejoice!

When God has a plan for your life, you will

not be able to fit in with everyone. You may not have many friends. You may even feel out of place in many atmospheres. I have rarely ever been able to fit in anywhere and I am sure there are those of you reading this book who feel the same way. Yet, you have to remind yourself, "It is because of the call on my life"; "I am destined for greatness"; "My life has purpose". In John Chapter 4, Jesus went through Samaria where he met a woman at the well. She did not realize that she was talking to Jesus, the Son of God. Yet, after a brief conversation, Jesus, in so many words, said, "Woman, if you only knew who I was..." The revelation is that there will be times when people do not recognize who you are in Christ. They fail to perceive the power in you, your greatness and your potential. They do not truly understand you, so they treat you differently and reject you.

CHAPTER 2

"EVERYBODY CAN'T GO"

There was a statement I once disliked hearing people say. The statement was, "Everybody can't go." It sounded so cliché, but the truth is, EVERYBODY CAN'T GO. One day a prophet prophesied to me and said, "There are some people you are trying to take with you, but God said they can't go." Tears welled up in my eyes because I knew that God was speaking to me, and trust me, letting go was not easy. I honestly did not want to let go and it took me months to do so. During those months, I experienced rejection from those same people who God said could not go. Now I realize that the rejection came as a result of my disobedience. I was afraid to let go. The longer I held on, the more miserable I became. I cried a lot, and many days I could not eat or sleep. God was allowing me to be miserable in that place because it was a place He no longer had for me. Then one day I finally made up in my mind to be obedient to the word that God had spoken: *"They can't go"*. And the day that I finally let go, my strength came back; the tears of rejection stopped flowing and I started smiling again. The POWER of

REJECTION!

God delivered me in my thinking one day when He asked me a question. He said, *"Ayannah, if everybody went, then why would I need to send you?"...* Wow! ...Think about that for yourself: If everybody went, then why would God need to send you? YOU are the chosen one. YOU are the sent one and the truth is, sometimes you have to go alone...Moses! Could it be that God has allowed rejection in your life so that He could get you alone? God wants to spend some one-on-one time with you. When Moses went to the mountain top of Mount Sinai in the book of Exodus Chapter 34, he went alone. God commanded him to come to the top of the mount and that no man should come with him. Being obedient to God's command, Moses was alone on that mountain and God met him there. The truth about going up on the mountain top with God is that while you are there, YOU CHANGE. And there will be times when people will not be able to handle your new changes. This brings about rejection. The Bible says that when Moses came down from the mountain top, his face was shining and radiant because he had been in the presence of the Almighty God. Moses' face had such a glow that Aaron and the children of Israel were afraid to come near him. The same thing happened when Jesus went up into a high mountain in Matthew Chapter 17. The Bible says that he was transfigured and his face did shine as the sun and his raiment (clothing) was white as the light. Though God is willing to change your circumstance, He is more interested in changing you. *"Therefore if any man be in Christ, he is a new creature: old things are passed away; behold, all things are become new"* (2 Corinthians 5:17 KJV). You are changing, and when you change, things change.

In the Bible when the angel of the Lord, Gabriel, appeared to Mary (the mother of Jesus) and said, *"Hail Mary, you are highly favored among all women"*, it was clear that he was letting Mary know that she was chosen and picked out by God. Every woman was not selected to be the birth carrier of Jesus. Not every woman had the capacity to bring forth our Savior. However, amongst all women, Mary was chosen. God selected Mary for this great cause and God has selected YOU for a great cause. So again "**Moses**" and "**Mary**", everybody just cannot go. When there are too many people around you, **Gideon**, God begins to shift things. In the book of Judges (chapters 6 and 7), the angel of the Lord appeared before Gideon and referred to him as a "mighty man of valour". God was proclaiming to Gideon that there was a warrior hidden on the inside of him. And when the time of battle approached, the Bible states that the Lord said unto Gideon, *"The people that are with thee are too many…"* (Judges 7:2 KJV). Gideon had too many people around him. So God took him through a process where the number of people with Gideon began to decrease from 32,000 to 10,000 to 300. What a reduction! And with those 300 men, Gideon won the battle over the Midianites. Can I tell you that God wants to do more with less. Sometimes you do not need all 12 disciples around you; you only need three (Read Matthew 17:1). Many great leaders in the Bible were loners. It was because of the great call on their lives.

God wants you to be totally dependent on

Him and confident in His voice and His voice alone. My sheep know My voice and a stranger they will not follow (John 10:4-5). When there are too many human voices speaking and influencing you, God starts rearranging things. People begin to leave you, relationships begin to alter and friendships become different, but there is power in rejection! It is all a part of God's great plan for your life. So do not cry over anyone who left you. That person was not connected to your destiny. If it was meant for them to stay, God would have allowed them to stay. 1 John 2:19 (NIV) says, *"They went out from us, but they did not really belong to us. For if they had belonged to us, they would have remained with us; but their going showed that none of them belonged to us."* Let them go! We have to be cognizant of when it is time to let people go. Do not allow the wrong people to occupy a space that God has designed for the right people. The right people can not show up in your life until the wrong people have been removed.

CHAPTER 3

"REJECTION QUALIFIES YOU"

In 1 Samuel Chapter 15, King Saul disobeyed the commandments of the LORD and because of that, God sent the prophet, Samuel, to inform Saul of his transgressions. In submission to God's command, Samuel told Saul that because of his disobedience, God had rejected him as King over Israel. Here is what I find interesting. The Bible says in verse 35, *"And Samuel came no more to see Saul until the day of his death: nevertheless Samuel mourned for Saul."* Let us look at the first part of that scripture. After Samuel informed Saul of his transgressions, the scripture says that Samuel never saw Saul again. God put major separation between that which was accepted by God (Samuel) and that which was rejected by God (Saul). This means that some relationships/friendships alter and separate due to sin. Now let us review the second part of that scripture which reads, "...nevertheless, Samuel mourned for Saul." The MSG Bible says that Samuel grieved long and deeply over him. Here we see that the prophet Samuel expressed sorrow and grief over his disconnection from Saul. This part of the scripture reveals that in times of rejection and separation, a person may experience feelings of sadness and grief, but here is where this story takes a turn. In 1 Samuel 16:1 (KJV), God asks Samuel a question: *"How long wilt thou mourn for Saul, seeing I have rejected him from reigning over Israel?"* God was saying to Samuel, "you have mourned over Saul long enough; I have rejected him." The Holy Ghost told me to ask you a question. "How long will you mourn over that relationship, over that friendship, over that business deal, over that house, over that job or over that person, seeing as though God has rejected it out of your life?" Stop right here and let that sink in your spirit. As I am writing this book, God is dealing with me also because there have been situations where I just absolutely mourned too long. Trust me, some of the same experiences that you have had, I have experienced also. Even those great men and women in the Bible have experienced these things long before us.

After God had rejected Saul, God was ready to anoint a new king over Israel. God gave the prophet Samuel specific instructions to fill his horn with oil and to go to Jesse's house to anoint the next king (1 Samuel 16:1). When Jesse brought his seven sons in to see who would be selected as king, David, who was also Jesse's son, was not escorted in with his brothers and neither was he mentioned. No one even uttered David's name to be a part of the selection process. Now Samuel was a true prophet of God, yet he looked at Eliab, Jesse's son, and said, *"Surely this is the Lord's anointed."* God immediately corrected him and said, *"Look not on his countenance, or on the height of his stature; because I have refused him: for the LORD seeth not as man seeth; for man looketh on the outward appearance, but the LORD looketh on the heart"* (1 Samuel 16:7 KJV). After Samuel had viewed all seven of Jesse's sons, he told Jesse that the LORD had not chosen any of these. Samuel then asked Jesse, ***"Is there another son?"***. Glory to God, the Lord just dropped this in my spirit for someone reading this book. There is going to come a time that after that employer on that job has looked through every application and every resume, they are going to ask, **"Is there another one?"** I decree and declare in the name of Jesus that the person they are looking for is YOU. I felt that! The Bible goes on to say that Samuel sent for David and when David appeared, God Himself spoke and said, *"Arise, anoint him: for this is he"* (1 Samuel 16:12 KJV). Samuel anointed David in the midst of his brothers and the Spirit of the LORD came upon David from that day forward. What I am trying to help you see is that there will be times when people overlook you, count you out and exclude you from the lineup; however, in actuality, you are the one God Himself has chosen, and He is going to allow His purpose to be fulfilled in the presence of those who thought that others were better than you and more qualified than you. You have to be rejected in order to be selected. Let me say that again, you have to be rejected in order to be selected. Rejection is what qualifies you. *"Then Jesus asked them, "Didn't you ever read this in the Scriptures? 'The stone that the builders rejected has now become the cornerstone. This is the LORD's doing, and it is wonderful to see"* (Matthew 21:42 NLT). This is the LORD's doing! The power of rejection! Today, let us be delivered from the opinions of people. God made it clear that man's opinion does not affect His decision. Man looks at the outer appearance but God does not see things the way that we see things. Isaiah 55:8-9 (KJV) God declares, *"For my thoughts are not your thoughts, neither are your ways my ways, saith the LORD. For as the heavens are higher than the earth, so are my ways higher than your ways, and my thoughts than your thoughts."* God is ready to anoint you as the next _____ (fill in the blank). Are you ready?

CHAPTER 4

"COME OUT FROM AMONG THEM"

You may still be wondering, how is there power in rejection. Here is how. Rejection brings spiritual awareness that you are about to be promoted and elevated. It is a sign of transition and that God is positioning you for your next level and dimension. Let us take an in depth look at the biblical life of Joseph, who experienced rejection throughout the early years of his life. Whenever Joseph's name is mentioned, we think of him as a "dreamer" who told his dreams, got thrown into a pit, sold into slavery and later became the ruler of Egypt. All of this is true, but if we ever look at Joseph's life more closely, we will see that GOD strategically used REJECTION all throughout Joseph's life to bring him into a place of prominence, wealth and leadership. Let's go deeper. (I pray that this revelation blesses your life just as it has blessed mine.)

Genesis Chapter 37, the account of Joseph's life, immediately begins in verse two by telling us that Joseph brought unto his father the evil report of his brothers. The Bible mentions that Joseph's brothers did wickedness in the sight of the Lord. God clearly made a distinction between Joseph, being of good report and his brothers, being of evil report. The truth about rejection is that it will often come from those whom you love and are close to. But here is how rejection is powerful. God removes people out of your life so that they will not contaminate you and cause you to do evil in the sight of the Lord. God did not want Joseph to be influenced and contaminated by his brothers or his environment, so God began to use rejection to move Joseph out of one place into another. His tumultuous experience was all because of the great call that God had on Joseph's life to one day be the ruler of Egypt. Take a look at your surroundings. Are you amongst people who have the potential to cause you to do evil in the sight of the Lord?

Keep the following Bible verses in mind: 1 Corinthians 15:33 (KJV) says, *"Be not deceived: evil communications corrupt good manners."* The NIV says it another way, *"Do not be misled: Bad company corrupts good character."* Separation is often required in certain situations to protect your character, your reputation and most importantly, your anointing. Second Corinthians 6:17 (KJV) declares, *"Come out from among them, and be ye separate, saith the Lord, and touch not the unclean thing; and I will receive you."* God often uses rejection to move you out of one place, into the place He has for you. Joseph was rejected by his brothers, but he was accepted by God. Which would you prefer: the acceptance of man or the acceptance of God? The beauty of it is that God loves us enough not to let us get too overly entangled in the wrong situations and with the wrong people for too long.

The Scripture also reveals to us that Joseph's brothers were extremely envious and jealous of him, and the truth about jealousy is that it is an evil and vicious spirit. James 3:16 (NLT) states, *"For wherever there is jealousy and selfish ambition, there you will find disorder and evil of every kind."* In Joseph's case, God had to move him away from his brothers by using rejection because his brother's envy and jealousy caused them to have deadly intentions towards Joseph. His own brothers plotted to kill him. What the enemy was truly after was to destroy the dreams and the call that God had upon Joseph's life. The attack was not against the man, the attack was against his mantle. That just blessed me! Let me say that again, the attack was not against the man, the attack was against his mantle, his calling, his destiny. The enemy uses people to reject you in order to wound you and hinder you because he fears you. He fears your God-given power and authority. People reject you because they cannot control you. They will only do to you what you allow them to do. They are intimidated by your intelligence, your thinking, your ideas, your ambition, your creativity, your power and your anointing. Sometimes the glory of God on your life is way too strong for the enemy to handle, so he sends anything and anyone to block you, hinder you and ultimately take you out. Ephesians 6:12 (KJV) declares, *"For we wrestle not against flesh and blood, but against principalities, against powers, against the rulers of darkness of this world, against spiritual wickedness in high places."* But I am here to declare that *"No weapon that is formed against thee shall prosper"* (Isaiah 54:17 KJV). *"For God hath not given us the spirit of fear; but of power, and of love, and of a sound mind"* (2 Timothy 1:7 KJV). The dreams and visions that God has shown you shall come to pass!

Surely you see that what you are going through is all a part of God's plan. First Thessalonians 5:18 (KJV) tells us that *"In every thing give thanks: for this is the will of God in Christ Jesus concerning you."* So instead of crying because someone left you, or because the job did not hire you, or because your parents did not accept you, begin to thank God. When you thank God in EVERYTHING, as 1 Thessalonians 5:18 tells us to do, you take the power away from the enemy and begin giving God the glory for your life. You strip the enemy of his weapons when you begin to thank God in spite of your circumstances. So begin to say, "Lord I thank You that they rejected me; I thank You that I did not get the job; I thank You that I was not accepted; I thank You that my parents did not love me; I thank You that my spouse divorced me; I thank You that my friends excluded me. Father I thank You." See what we just did. We just tore down the strongholds of Satan and began giving God praise for EVERYTHING that has happened to us. Romans 8:28 (KJV) says, *"And we KNOW that ALL things work together for good to them that love God, to them who are the called according to his purpose."* God never meant for it to destroy you. In Jeremiah 29:11 (KJV), God declares, *"For I know the thoughts that I think toward you, saith the LORD, thoughts of peace, and not of evil, to give you an expected end."* When you recognize that God is in control of it all, your appetite will come back; you will be able to sleep at night; you will dry your tears and declare that if God be for me, who can be against me. It is working together for your good.

CHAPTER 5

"GOD IS WITH YOU"

Let's go deeper. Joseph's brothers, being extremely jealous of him, decided to throw Joseph into a pit and sell him into slavery. He was sold to the Ishmaelites for 20 pieces of silver and was carried away into Egypt. In Egypt, he was sold unto Potiphar who was an officer of Pharaoh. But even in bondage, the mantle, the anointing and the call was still upon Joseph's life. The Bible made note in Genesis 39:2 that the Lord was with Joseph. Let us pause right here and consider that note. Even in the midst of being rejected by his brothers, thrown into a pit, sold into slavery and carried into another country to be a slave under Potiphar, the Bible says that the Lord was with Joseph. The scripture comes to mind, *"When thou passest through the waters, I will be with thee; and through the rivers, they shall not overflow thee: when thou walkest through the fire, thou shall not be burned; neither shall the flame kindle upon thee"* (Isaiah 43:2 KJV). As for you, that means that even though rejection has seemingly put you in a bad place, you can be confident that in that place, the Lord is with you. The Bible mentions in that same passage of scripture (Genesis 39:2) that

Joseph was a prosperous man. How is it that Joseph is a "slave", yet the Bible declares him as a prosperous man? How can a slave in bondage be prosperous? It was because the Lord was with him.

The Bible goes on to point out in Genesis 39 that Potiphar saw that the Lord was with Joseph and that the Lord caused all that Joseph did to prosper. Here is another nugget: Be around people who can see God in you, who can recognize your greatness and people who do not mind celebrating you. When Potiphar noticed the greatness in Joseph, he celebrated him by giving him a position in his house. He made Joseph overseer of his dwelling, and put into his hand, all that he owned. Potiphar recognized Joseph's favor with God and accommodated the anointing on Joseph's life. The same thing happened in 2 Kings Chapter 4. The Shunammite woman recognized that Elisha was a holy man of God (verse 9), and because of that, she and her husband created a space for Elisha in their home. The anointing that is on your life is valuable and God wants you in a place where it is protected and honored. When people no longer honor your anointing, you have to get going. Never become so familiar with people to a point where you are no longer able to lead them and be of a Godly influence to them.

Side note: A prophet once told me that it is important to be around people who are five years ahead of you. If you are the smartest person in your circle, then your circle is too small. And ultimately that means that your circle can not advance you. You have to be in the midst of people who can ignite you, propel you and push you into the place that God is wanting to take you. It is important to be amongst people who have the same type of drive and aspirations that you have. If you do not surround yourself with these types of individuals, your growth will be stunted and your progress will be stagnated. Proverbs 27:17 (KJV) declares, *"Iron sharpeneth iron; so a man sharpeneth the countenance of his friend."*

Now back to Joseph. Though Potiphar noticed the hand of God on Joseph's life, the truth is that Joseph could not stay under Potiphar forever. Remember, there was a mandate on Joseph's life to one day be a ruler himself. So as for you, do not get comfortable where you are. You are not destined to remain positioned there forever. When God rejects you out of a place, it means that you can no longer thrive in that environment. That place has served its purpose and it is now time for you to move on.

CHAPTER 6

"TESTING SIGNIFIES A PROMOTION"

As mentioned before in Chapter 4, the enemy is after the mantle, and the heaviness of your mantle determines the heaviness of your tests. Testing must come before you are promoted into your next level and dimension. In these tests, God proves your authority over the enemy. Before Job received double, he was tested (Job Chapters 1 and 2). He lost everything, including his children. Before David was made King over Israel, he was tested. Saul pursued David for a great period of time to try to kill him (1 Samuel 23:13-17). Before Jesus went forth in his ministry, he was tested. The Bible says that Jesus was led up of the Spirit into the wilderness to be tempted of the devil (Matthew 4). Did you catch that? The Spirit of God led Jesus into the wilderness to be tested. This means that the tests in your life are God ordained; they have purpose. In Luke 22:31-32 (KJV), Jesus tells Simon (Peter), *"Simon, Simon, behold, Satan hath desired to have you, that he may sift you as wheat: But I have prayed for thee, that thy faith fail not: and when thou art converted, strengthen thy brethren."* Jesus never prayed that Simon would not go through the test. He prayed that his faith would not fail him during the test. The purpose of Simon going through the test was so that once he came out, his spirit would be strengthened in order to properly deal with his brethren spiritually. In other words, the test would give Simon (Peter) a testimony that would help others. Can you think of a test that you have gone through, and once you came out of it, you had a powerful testimony that could help someone else? Testing is necessary because it purges the intent of man and brings forth a greater level of obedience. In Hebrews 5:8, the Bible declares that Jesus learned obedience through the things he suffered. Suffering is required because obedience is mandatory.

Keep in mind that elevation means to move or raise to a higher place or position, both naturally and spiritually. With this being said, there will always be a face to face battle with Satan before you are elevated. Before Joseph could reign as the ruler of Egypt, he had to be tested. God again had to use rejection to transition and reposition Joseph. Though the Spirit of God was with Joseph at Potiphar's house, the spirit of the enemy was still present to destroy the dreams. In this case, Joseph's test came when Potiphar's wife began to pursue him. God wanted to see how Joseph would respond. Joseph refused Potiphar's wife and made this powerful statement. He said, "How then can I do this great wickedness, and sin against God?" (Genesis 39:9 KJV). Joseph took a stand against evil in order to be blameless and pure before the Lord, and when he refused her, she lied on him and accused him of trying to force himself upon her. This in turn, caused Potiphar to angrily turn against Joseph, reject him and have him thrown in prison. Now let us take a look at this situation. Potiphar had entrusted everything he had unto Joseph. He knew that Joseph was a man of integrity and that Joseph could be trusted. He was very aware of the fact that the hand of God was upon Joseph's life. So why would Potiphar believe such an accusation against Joseph? Bear in mind, accusations come from the enemy and Satan is the accuser of the brethren (Revelation 12:10). The truth is, this was Joseph's test. Joseph had to be lied on and rejected. God was preparing him to be ushered into his next dimension. His season was up at Potiphar's house.

Could it be that the accusations and rejection that you have faced or may be facing is because your season is up in a place? We must keep in mind that the LORD showed Joseph in his dreams that he would be a high authoritative figure in leadership and power. He never showed Joseph himself being a slave and in bondage. Yet, all of this was a part of the process to lead Joseph into his destiny. Even though Joseph was prospering at Potiphar's house, that was not the ultimate vision that God had shown him. Though you may be prospering where you are, it is possible that that is not the place God ultimately showed you. In order to get you to the place that God has shown you, sometimes He allows chaos to occur in your life to push you into the place that He has for you.

Transition often comes through trials. And most transitions are very uncomfortable while most trials test the inner core of who you are. Job

23:10 (KJV) says it best: *"But he knoweth the way that I take: when he hath tried me, I shall come forth as gold."* God knows which way you are headed, so let the fire of your trials purify you as pure gold. *"Behold, I have refined thee, but not with silver; I have chosen thee in the furnace of affliction"* (Isaiah 48:10 KJV). Isaiah 48 says that we are refined in the FURNACE of affliction. Affliction is already a state of pain, distress or grief, but a furnace is a place of intense heat, which means, God takes us through a fiery, intense place of pain in order to purify us. First Peter 4:12-13 (KJV) says, *"Beloved, think it not strange concerning the fiery trial which is to try you, as though some strange thing happened unto you: But rejoice, inasmuch as ye are partakers of Christ's sufferings; that, when his glory shall be revealed, ye may be glad also with exceeding joy."* Look at Job. The Bible says in Job 1:20 that after Satan had launched a full blown attack on Job, Job fell to the ground and worshipped God. When Job worshipped God, it took all of the power away from Satan and gave God total glory. We often say, "God we give You all the glory", but are we truly giving God ALL the glory for even the bad events that happen in our lives?

Despite what happens, be sure that when God moves you out of the place you are in - that you leave with your hands clean and your heart pure. Be confident that you have done everything to the best of your ability to make peace. This way you can assuredly say, "I was the best mother/father that I could be; I was the best son/daughter that I could be; I was the best friend that I could be; I was the best employee that I could be; or I was the best person that I could be." Joseph had done nothing wrong and because of that, he was able to walk away from Potiphar's house knowing that he had done what was right in the sight of the Lord. He passed his test!

CHAPTER 7

"YOUR GIFT WILL MAKE ROOM FOR YOU"

Despite the fact that Potiphar's wife accused Joseph and caused him to be wrongfully sent to prison, the Bible makes sure to mention that God was still with Joseph. Think on that. Even in prison, God was still with him. Joseph's rejection at Potiphar's house caused him to be in a place where his gift would ultimately make room for him and bring him before great men (Proverbs 18:16). Can I announce to you that rejection is a divine set-up to get you where God wants you to be! It allows your God-given gift to have the ability to make room for you. So the next time someone rejects you, do not cry. Rejoice that you are headed in the right direction with God, and though you may not see it or understand it, be confident that it is working together for your good.

God orchestrated for Joseph to be incarcerated because it would unlock a door that would catapult him into the place that God had prepared for him. Let me prophesy to you that it is when you are in your valley, your low place, your prison experience, that your gift will make room for you. It is after you have been rejected, ostracized, left out, overlooked, cast aside and forgotten about that God can open a door for you that was shut. It is when you are broken, weak, discouraged and defeated that God can make a way out of no way. When David cried out unto the Lord in Psalm 18, the Bible says that the earth shook and God came down to see about David. And let us never forget that we serve that same God. He is the same yesterday, today and forever. Glory to God! (I would like to make mention that as I am writing this book, I feel the anointing of God).

Joseph was in a low, rejected place and I am more than sure that he cried many nights. He suffered the heartache of being rejected and ostracized by his own family at a young age. He endured the pain of being lied on by Potiphar's wife and withstood the rejection of Potiphar, a man he faithfully honored. Yet, God still had a plan.

While in prison, Joseph was given an opportunity by God to interpret the dreams of the butler and the baker, who had also been imprisoned. These two men were officers under Pharaoh, the King of Egypt. (If we were in church right now, I would tell you to tell your neighbor, "It's a set-up"). One particular night, the butler and the baker both had a dream, yet there was no one to interpret the dreams. But God had strategically placed Joseph in position to be able to properly interpret the dreams individually for each man. In this, God was allowing Joseph's gift to be revealed. After interpreting the dreams, Joseph made one request to the butler. He asked the butler to remember him and to make mention of him to Pharaoh. Genesis 40:23 (KJV) says, *"Yet did not the chief butler remember Joseph, but forgat him."* I believe that it was God's divine plan for the butler to forget Joseph because it was not yet Joseph's appointed time to be fully released into his destiny. We must always keep in mind that God's timing is perfect and anything outside of God's timing can cause you to prematurely abort your destiny.

It later came a time when Pharaoh, the King of Egypt, dreamed a two part dream (Genesis 41). The Bible says that he called all the magicians of Egypt and all the wise men, but there was no one who could interpret his dream. It was then, at that appointed time, that the butler remembered Joseph and mentioned to Pharaoh that Joseph had interpreted his dream while he was in prison. Pharaoh immediately sent for Joseph. When Joseph arrived, there in that very moment, he was able to interpret Pharaoh's dream. Joseph even offered Pharaoh wisdom as to how to properly prepare for the seven good years of plenteous and the seven years of famine that God had shown Pharaoh in his dream. What is interesting in this passage of scripture is that once Joseph interpreted the dreams and offered wisdom and solutions as to what Pharaoh should do, the Bible mentions that Pharaoh asked his servants a question: "Can we find anyone else like this man so obviously filled with the Spirit of God?" Take a deep look at this. Pharaoh, a **nonbeliever**, acknowledged the One and True Living God. I speak that God is going to anoint your giftings and calling so strongly, that even those who do not believe will have to acknowledge our God.

Pharaoh was so impressed by the wisdom that God had granted Joseph that in that very same moment, he made Joseph ruler over his house and over all the land of Egypt. I want to prophesy to you that though you were overlooked and forgotten about, you are next in line for a promotion. Psalm 75:6-7 (KJV) declares, *"For promotion cometh neither from the east, nor from the west, nor from the south. But God is the judge: he putteth down one, and setteth up another."* God has not forgotten about you. Overnight, Joseph went from being a rejected slave and prisoner to being the ruler of Egypt. Did you catch that? OVERNIGHT! I prophesy in the name of Jesus that at God's appointed time in your life, things will begin to happen for you overnight! You are going to go to bed one night as a prisoner and you are going to wake up the next day in the position that God has for you. You are going to go to bed one night feeling rejected, but you are going to wake up the next morning feeling empowered. You are going to go to bed one night broke and wake up the next day wealthy. You are going to go to bed one night a nobody and wake up the next morning and your name will be great. It was good for you that you were overlooked and cast out. It was good for you that people rejected you. It was good for you that you did not get that job. It was good for you that you were denied that loan. It was good for you that your friends walked away from you. It was good for you that your family did not receive you. It was good for you that your mother or your father was not there. Psalm 27:10 (KJV) declares, *"When my father and my mother forsake me, then the Lord will take me up."* It is when you have been forsaken by man that God can take you "UP". All these things have helped to shape and mold you into the person that God wants you to be. So be very glad for the process that God has taken you through, for He knows where you are and where He wants to lead you.

I pray that by now you can see the power of rejection - the power when people walk away from you and leave you abandoned. Your life did not end when they left. Your life has just begun. Your testimony, your ministry, and your breakthrough has just begun. You just got your life back! You just got your power back!

Oftentimes, we give Satan way too much credit for things that are actually a part of the will of God. What do I mean? Could it be that it was Potiphar's wife's assignment to accuse Joseph so that he would end up in prison? There is no doubt that Satan was involved and caused her to do these things, but I am a firm believer that God allowed it to happen this way to reposition Joseph for his next level. How else would Joseph have ended up in prison to be in place to interpret those dreams? See, it was in prison that Joseph's gift of dream interpretation was able to bring him before Pharaoh and cause him to be crowned the ruler of Egypt. So why then be mad at Potiphar's wife? She was only carrying out her assignment. Jesus knew that Judas would betray Him and yet He still called him "friend". To call Judas "friend" always blows my mind! Nevertheless, Judas had to betray Jesus because it was his assignment. Judas' betrayal was a part of God's ultimate plan that would lead Jesus to the cross. So in essence, why are we upset with people when they are only carrying out their assignment? Forgive them, love them and move forward. Begin to give God glory for even the things that He allows Satan to do to you.

I am a living witness that rejection has made me a better person. Because of the rejection I have experienced, I am able to write this book. Yes, rejection hurt me. Yes, it almost broke me down. Yes, I was depressed. Yes, I felt lonely. Yes, I felt like no one loved me. Yet, when I think about all of the people that my testimony is going to help set free, I count it all joy. When I think about all of the testimonies that will come from this book, I can rejoice in what I went through. I give God glory. I thank God it happened to me, and you should be rejoicing also. Rejection was never meant to break you down and destroy you; it was allowed and used by God to bring you into a place of greatness - a place of success in God. It was divinely orchestrated by God Himself to help push you into your divine destiny.

CHAPTER 8

"THE PURPOSE OF THE TABLE"

Let us examine another aspect of the power of rejection. Joseph was placed in a position of power and prominence as the ruler of Egypt. He was in charge over everything under Pharaoh. It was during the seven good years in Egypt that Joseph collected and stored food and grain in the cities. The Bible states that he stored so much grain and corn that it was like the sands of the sea and could not be measured. God had granted Joseph great wisdom to do so because the time of famine was approaching. After the seven good years ended, the seven years of famine began in Egypt and all over the face of the earth (Genesis 41:56). People from all countries came to Egypt to buy corn from Joseph. Even his brothers, who lived in the land of Canaan, came to buy grain and corn on several occasions. Joseph knew who his brothers were but he never revealed himself to them. Here is what is interesting. On one occasion in Genesis 43, Joseph's brothers came from the land of Canaan to buy grain. When Joseph saw them, he told his servant to cook a meal and "prepare" the table because his brothers would be eating with him that day. Keep in mind that Joseph still had not yet revealed to his brothers who he was. So the servant did as told and prepared the meal and the table, and the Bible says in verse 33 of that same chapter that at the table, Joseph's brothers were facing him. Did you catch that? A table was prepared in the face and presence of those who rejected Joseph. Here is the revelation that God gave me and I pray that you receive this in the name of Jesus. Psalm 23:5 (KJV) says, *"Thou "**preparest a table**" before me "**in the presence**" of mine enemies..."* Now, I always thought that the purpose of God preparing a table before me in the presence of my enemies was so that I could show my enemies that I made it without them. I wanted my enemies and those who had hurt me and abandoned me to know that I was doing just fine without them in my life. Perhaps this is how many of us feel when we hear and read that scripture, but God broke it down to me a few years ago in another way. He said, *"Ayannah, your enemies already know that you made it without them. They already know that you're doing fine without them in your life. So why would I need to prepare a table for the* *obvious?"*… What God was saying to me was, why prepare a table for something that people already see and know. People already know that you are blessed, so there is no need to prepare a table for that reason. He said, *"The reason I prepare a table before you in the presence of your enemies is so that YOU can feed them."* I pray in the name of Jesus that you just caught that! Remember, we serve a God of love, mercy and forgiveness. The purpose of the table is to love your enemies and show mercy and forgiveness to those who have wronged you. The table is designed for you to take care of the needs of others who may have abandoned you and left you with nothing. The table is prepared so that you can share the Word of God with others and tell them of the goodness of Jesus. Please let this revelation sink into your spirit. Jesus commanded us in Matthew 5:44 (KJV) to *"Love your enemies, bless them that curse you, do good to them that hate you, and pray for them which despitefully use you, and persecute you."* This scripture continues to say that when you do this, you are recognized as the children of your Father which is in heaven. It goes on to say that if you only love people that love you, then there is no reward for that. The reward is in genuinely loving people who have hurt you to the core. It is all about forgiveness.

You may ask, "What is the reward?" Well, let us recall Psalm 23:5 where the scripture says, *"Thou preparest a table before me in the presence of mine enemies."* If you continue reading that same verse, it states *"...thou anointest my head with oil; my cup runneth over."* If you noticed in that scripture, the "anointing with oil" and the "overflowing of the cup" did not come until **after** the table was prepared. What God is saying here is that after you have forgiven those who have hurt you, wronged you, used you, left you, and rejected you, now He can anoint you afresh and the blessings of the LORD can overtake you. *"The blessing of the LORD, it maketh rich, and he addeth no sorrow with it"* (Proverbs 10:22 KJV).

For Joseph, it all began with rejection. Joseph, at a young age, dreamed dreams that one day his family would bow to him. And because of his dreams, his brothers rejected him. They got rid of him by selling him into slavery. Nevertheless, here is the revelation that God gave me concerning you, myself and Joseph… The people that rejected you will one day have to see you again. And I prophesy that when they see you this time, your latter state will be so much greater than when they saw you in your former state. I decree in the name of Jesus that by the time they see you again, God will have blessed you so much so, that they will not be able to recognize you. Joseph's brothers thought they had gotten rid of Joseph for good. They thought they would never see him again and that his dreams would never come to pass. They ostracized him and rejected him. They left him for dead, but years later the day came that his brothers stood before him, and because God had blessed Joseph so well, his own brothers did not recognize him. They bowed before him just as God had shown Joseph in his dreams when he was only 17 years old. And once Joseph finally revealed himself to his brothers (Genesis 45:5 NLT), he told his brothers, *"Don't be upset, and don't be angry with yourselves for selling me to this place. It was God who sent me here ahead of you to preserve your lives."* Wow, what a profound statement! Joseph understood that everything that had happened to him was the will of God for his life, and because of that, Joseph showed forgiveness towards his brothers. Joseph understood that the perfect will of God caused him to experience rejection from his family. It was rejection that pushed Joseph into the place of promise. I decree in the name of Jesus that the rejection you have faced is pushing you into your place of promise. Had Joseph not experienced a series of rejections, he would have not been in the proper place for God to exalt him over a nation. He went from being a rejected slave to a ruler over a NATION! So ultimately, what Joseph went through was not even about him. It was about the livelihood of so many other people. Remember, he told his brothers, "God sent me ahead of you to preserve your lives." I speak that what you have gone through is not even about you. It is about the well being of other people. The things you have experienced are so that when you share your testimony with others, they will be saved, delivered and set free. May God get total glory out of your life. Let the pain of your rejection work together for your good.

CHAPTER 9

"THE POWER OF FORGIVENESS"

It is important that we not only realize the power of rejection, but also we must realize the power of forgiveness. Forgiveness is **commanded** by God. Matthew 6:14-15 (NLT) pleads, *"If you forgive those who sin against you, your Heavenly Father will forgive you. But if you refuse to forgive others, your Father will not forgive your sins."* We all need God's forgiveness. We have no room to be unforgiving towards others. Think about some of the things you have done that were not right in the sight of the Lord. Now think about if God chose not to forgive you. I do not know about you, but my life would be a total mess if God chose not to forgive me for my sins. So then why do we expect God to be forgiving towards us and yet we cannot forgive one another? First John 4:20 (NLT) says, *"If someone says, "I love God," but hates his brother/sister, that person is a liar; for if we don't love people we can see, how can we love God, whom we cannot see?"* Despite what people have done to you, please, please, please, forgive them. In John 13:34-35 (NLT), Jesus gives us a new commandment. He says, *"Love each other. Just as I have loved you, you should love each other. Your love for* *one another will prove to the world that you are my disciples."* Jesus did not say that our religion or our beliefs would prove that we are His disciples. He said it is our love for one another that would prove that we are His disciples.

So if you are struggling with forgiving someone, make up in your mind RIGHT NOW that you choose to forgive them. Even if they NEVER apologize to you, you are commanded to forgive. Forgiveness is a choice. Say out loud, "In the name of Jesus, I choose to forgive _____" (Insert that person's name). Say it again, "In the name of Jesus, I choose to forgive _____." Cry if you have to, but it is time for you to be healed, in the name of Jesus. You have carried that burden long enough. It is time to cast your cares upon the LORD, because He cares for you (1 Peter 5:7).

There was one occasion in my life where I had to do this same exercise. I was struggling with forgiving someone who had never apologized to me for the way they treated me. And I had to say out loud to myself over and

over again, "I choose to forgive _____".
Every time the enemy would remind me of what
they did to me, I would say out loud, "I choose
to forgive _____". As often as the hurt
would pop up, I would say, "I choose to forgive
_____". Eventually, without even
noticing it, the pain gradually went away. And
now, years later, I barely remember what I was
trying to forgive them for. See, God has given us
authority in our mouths. When you speak words
out loud, you create an atmosphere. Remember,
"In the beginning" (Genesis Chapter 1), God
"spoke" and things were created, and we have
that same power to create things and
atmospheres with our words. *"Death and life are in
the power of the tongue: and they that love it shall eat the
fruit thereof"* (Proverbs 18:21 KJV). So we must
daily speak forgiveness. I am pleading with you to
PLEASE forgive those who have rejected you,
hurt you, left you, talked about you, abandoned
you, lied to you, lied on you, etc. You deserve to
be free. When you cannot forgive, you become
the prisoner, and I am a firm believer that
unforgiveness robs you of enjoying the abundant

life that Jesus desires for you to have.

Furthermore, now that you understand the blessings that come with rejection, you should **never** try to seek revenge or get even with someone who has wronged you. As a matter of fact, release that out of your mind. You **cannot** do unto others as they have done unto you. Remember, we will be held accountable individually for every deed done in this body whether good or bad (2 Corinthians 5:10). God is watching everything that we do. *"The eyes of the LORD are in every place, beholding the evil and the good"* Proverbs 15:3 (KJV).

In closing, I want to leave you with this passage of scripture that is so very powerful. Romans 12:17-21 (NIV): *"Do not repay anyone evil for evil. Be careful to do what is right in the eyes of everyone. If it is possible, as far as it depends on you, live at peace with everyone. Do not take revenge, my dear friends, but leave room for God's wrath, for it is written: "It is mine to avenge; I will repay," says the Lord. On the contrary: "If your enemy is hungry, feed him; if he is thirsty, give him something to drink. In doing this, you will heap burning coals on his head. Do not be overcome by evil, but overcome evil with good."* Joseph made up in his mind to do good unto his brothers who had done him wrong. Though he had spent a great segment of his life separated from his family, in the end, he invited them to come share in his portion. He shared the blessings of God with his family.

I pray that the revelation that God has given me while writing this book has blessed your life and has set you free in areas that you may have been bound. I believe that after reading this book, you will no longer look at rejection the same. You will no longer see rejection in a negative aspect, but you will begin to give God total glory for everything that has happened in your life. Remember, God is trying to push you into your divine destiny. He wants to bless you beyond measure. He loves you with an everlasting love. His plans for you are of good and not evil. No longer will we cry because we have been rejected, for now we know the POWER of REJECTION!

"A Declaration for Your Life"

Before I end this book, I want to pray and decree some things over you in the name of Jesus. I decree and declare by the power and authority given to me through Christ Jesus that you no longer hold on to the things that people have done to you. In the name of Jesus, release everything. Release unforgiveness; release resentment; release what they said to you; release how they treated you. Every hurt, every pain and every negative thought, release it now in the name of Jesus, for He binds up the wounds of the brokenhearted. In Jesus' name, I bind the spirit of sadness and depression, the spirit of hurt and fear, the spirit of give-up and give-out. For whatsoever we bind on earth is already bound in Heaven. In the name of Jesus, I reject the spirit of rejection that was sent by the enemy to destroy you. I crush the spirit of low self-esteem and the spirit of "not good enough". I curse the spirit of suicide at the root. I break the bands of loneliness and isolation. I rebuke every word spoken over you that you would never be anything. I reject every negative utterance spoken over you and against you. I sever the ties of ungodly relationships and friendships. I command the cycles to be broken, in the name of Jesus. No more going in circles over and over again. In the name of Jesus we put an end to it this day. I decree that you will be happy again. I decree that you will love again. I decree that the right people will come into your life. I speak blessings over your life. I speak peace over your life. I speak healing over your life; healing over your mind and emotions. By faith your life shall be restored. Now, roll the stone away and take the grave clothes off because it is time for you to live again. In the name of Jesus, receive power; receive strength; receive your new beginning. You are being revived, restored and refreshed. In Jesus' mighty name and it is so. Amen.

"THE POWER OF REJECTION"

Stay Connected!

www.ayannahwilliamsministries.com

AYANNAH WILLIAMS MINISTRIES

www.ayannahwilliamsministries.com

**Be sure to visit me online at
ayannahwilliamsministries.com!**

**Sermon Clips · Speaking Engagements Schedule ·
Order Books · Prayer Requests … and more!**

facebook.com/MinisterAyannahWilliams

@MinisterAyannah

@Ayannah_Williams

www.ingramcontent.com/pod-product-compliance
Lightning Source LLC
Chambersburg PA
CBHW062024040426
42447CB00010B/2122

*9 7 8 0 9 9 7 3 9 9 6 1 5 *